NORTHUMBRIA IN PICTURES

A Colour Souvenir

For John, who made this book possible, and in memory
of my parents.

ACKNOWLEDGEMENTS

The publishers wish to thank all the individuals and organisations who have been involved in the production of 'Northumbria in Pictures' - those who supplied copy and photographs, those responsible for design, and those who supported the project with their enthusiasm.

To Her Grace The Duchess of Northumberland for consenting to write the 'Foreword'.

In particular, appreciation is due to Peter Reynolds of Bernicia Photography, who travelled so many miles in search of the perfect conditions for his pictures, and with whom the weather so rarely co-operated!

And to John Kimber, from Cowells, our thanks for his unfailing courtesy and helpful guidance.

Finally, to the many writers whose books (too numerous to list) were consulted to verify facts.

Photographic credits

Nos. 1-2, 6-12, 14-17, 20, 29, 34-35, 38	Bernicia Photography.
Nos. 3-5	City of Newcastle upon Tyne.
Nos. 13 & 30	Airfotos.
No. 18	Ernest Storey.
Nos. 19, 21-22, 27, 37, 39	Northumbria Tourist Board.
No. 23	National Trust.
No. 24	Vindolanda Trust.
Nos. 25-26	Hexham Tourist Information Centre.
No. 28	Northumberland County Council.
Nos. 31-32	Durham County Council.
No. 33	Borough of South Tyneside.
No. 36	Beamish Museum.
No. 40	Sunderland Borough Council.

NORTHUMBRIA IN PICTURES

A Colour Souvenir compiled by Beryl Scott.

FOREWORD BY HER GRACE THE DUCHESS OF NORTHUMBERLAND

First published in Great Britain in 1986.

Sandhill Press Ltd., Castleside, 40, Narrowgate,
Alnwick, Northumberland, NE66 1JQ.

ISBN 0 946098 04 2

Printed in Great Britain by W. S. Cowell Ltd.,
8 Butter Market, Ipswich, Suffolk

FOREWORD

For many years there has been no hardback book of good colour photographs of Northumberland, Tyne & Wear, and Durham. This ommission is all the more regrettable in view of the large number of illustrated books which are published about other areas of the country.

I am delighted that the Sandhill Press has now remedied the deficiency, and have great pleasure in commending this book to all those who love Northumbria, be they first-time visitors or longstanding inhabitants.

Elizabeth Northumberland

IN PICTURES
NORTHUMBRIA

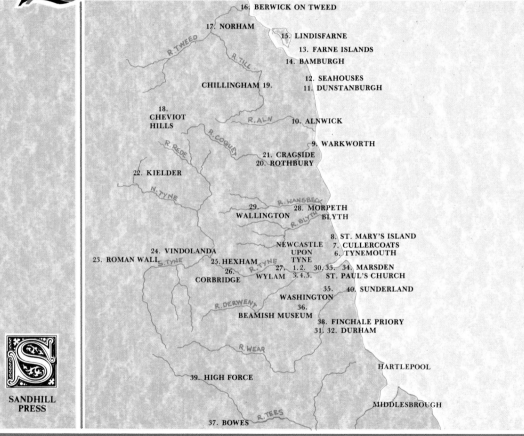

16. BERWICK ON TWEED

17. NORHAM

15. LINDISFARNE

13. FARNE ISLANDS

14. BAMBURGH

CHILLINGHAM 19.

12. SEAHOUSES
11. DUNSTANBURGH

18. CHEVIOT HILLS

10. ALNWICK

9. WARKWORTH

21. CRAGSIDE
20. ROTHBURY

22. KIELDER

29. WALLINGTON

28. MORPETH
BLYTH

24. VINDOLANDA

23. ROMAN WALL

8. ST. MARY'S ISLAND
7. CULLERCOATS
6. TYNEMOUTH

NEWCASTLE UPON TYNE

25. HEXHAM

26. CORBRIDGE

27. WYLAM

1. 2. 30. 33. 34. MARSDEN
3. 4. 5. ST. PAUL'S CHURCH

35. 40. SUNDERLAND

36. WASHINGTON

BEAMISH MUSEUM

38. FINCHALE PRIORY

31. 32. DURHAM

HARTLEPOOL

39. HIGH FORCE

MIDDLESBROUGH

37. BOWES

SANDHILL PRESS

CONTENTS

THE TYNE BRIDGE.

Well-known throughout the world, the sight of the great span of the Tyne Bridge welcomes travellers to Newcastle upon Tyne, the busy regional capital of the north east. The bridge, with the largest arch of its type in the country, was built by Dorman Long of Middlesbrough and opened in 1928 by King George V. It was used as a model for the Sydney Harbour Bridge in Australia which was built by the same company.

The site of Newcastle upon Tyne has been of strategic importance for centuries and the first bridge to cross its river was 'Pons Aelius' built by the Roman Legionnaires. The present Swing Bridge, designed by Lord Armstrong, stands on the same site and uses hydraulic machinery to pivot the central section and allow shipping to pass along the river.

Six bridges in all now cross the river here, the others being:
The High Level Bridge, designed by Robert Stephenson and opened by Queen Victoria in 1849, it carries vehicles on its lower level and a railway line above.
Queen Elizabeth II Bridge opened by Her Majesty in 1981 to carry the new Metro Passenger Transport system.
King Edward VII Bridge which was built in 1906 and carries the Edinburgh to London railway line. Redheugh Bridge, first built in 1901, the new replacement bridge was opened by Princess Diana in 1983.

Below these bridges, along the Quayside, are some of the oldest buildings in the 2,000 year history of the City, many of which are now being revitalised. On Sundays the Quayside is the scene of an interesting open-air market of some two hundred stalls.

1. THE TYNE BRIDGE
Newcastle upon Tyne

ST. NICHOLAS CATHEDRAL.

The original parish church of St. Nicholas became a cathedral in 1882 when the Diocese of Newcastle was established. The Norman building was largely destroyed by two fires in 1216 and 1248, but from money raised, these ruins were pulled down and the new structure with its graceful pointed arches and slender piers took shape.

The most striking feature of the Cathedral, the Lantern Tower, was added in 1448. This was the gift of Robert Rhodes, a Newcastle citizen between 1427 and 1473, who represented the City at parliament. The inscription (translated) "pray for the soul of Robert Rhodes" is to be found in the vaulting of the tower, just above the font. Described by Mackenzie in 1827 as "one of the noblest and admired structures in our island" the Tower is 196½ feet from its base to the top of the steeple, and upon its four buttresses stand statues representing Adam, Eve, Aaron and David.

It is traditionally held to be the work of a Dominican lay brother, who as a reward for his remarkable skill, was given the privilege of singing Mass once a year in the church. The spire was believed to be saved from destruction in the siege of 1644 by the Mayor, Sir John Marley, who put Scottish prisoners in the Tower to stop the attacking artillery fire of the enemy.

At the south east end of the nave inside the church is a magnificent brass lectern. The only Pre-Reformation lectern in the north-east, it dates from the 16th century and shows a brass figure of an eagle resting on a sphere. It is a memorial to Roger Thornton, a merchant, Mayor and benefactor of the City.

2. ST. NICHOLAS CATHEDRAL
Newcastle upon Tyne

THE CASTLE AND KEEP.

The ancient city and port of Newcastle upon Tyne has much of its visible and recorded history dating from Norman times. The 'New Castle' was built in 1080 A.D. by Robert Curthose, the eldest son of William the Conqueror. The fortifications of the town in the 13th century recognised its military value. From then on the castle was strengthened on many occasions because of the bitter border conflicts. Originally made from wood, then reinforced by stone, Henry II began another castle on the same site in 1168, and the Castle Keep was built by him between 1171 and 1172.

The walls of the Keep were 18 feet thick, one of the finest examples of a Norman Keep in Britain. The main entrance, a decorated Norman arch, was restored in 1847 as an exact replica of the original using drawings by John Dobson. Now preserved as a museum by the Society of Antiquaries, it is open to the public.

Henry III built the adjacent 'Black Gate' in 1247 to protect the only level approach to the castle. Later replaced in 1618, its name derives from Patrick Black who lived there in 1640. Today it houses the world's only Bagpipe Museum and is open to the public.

The original walls of the city were last prepared for defence during the Jacobite Rebellion of 1745.

Remains of the West Walls, built by the Burgesses in the 13th century, still survive, as do Morden, Heber and Durham Towers.

Guided walks are available around all the historic remains of the City and Newcastle City Council produces excellent booklets to aid the visitor.

3. THE CASTLE AND KEEP
Newcastle upon Tyne

13

THE CIVIC CENTRE.

The ceremonial and administrative headquarters of Newcastle upon Tyne, the building was opened in 1968 by King Olav V of Norway. Designed by the then city architect, George Kenyon, it incorporates several interesting architectural features.

An impressive sight when floodlit, the outstanding Lantern Tower with its crest of sea horses and castles, stands silhouetted against the City skyline. A carillon of bells play local and seasonal tunes on special occasions. The famous River-God Tyne statue by David Wynne is the biggest piece of modern bronze sculpture in the country. He also designed the bronze 'Swans in Flight' formation in the quadrangle. The circular Council Chamber is raised on stilts over the Ceremonial Way and flanked by a row of nine flambeaux sculpted by Charles Sansbury.

Close-by, set in its own charming and tranquil grounds just two minutes from Newcastle's busy shopping area, is the Church of St. Thomas the Martyr. The original chapel built to honour his memory stood at the north-east corner of the old Roman Bridge (site of the present day Swing Bridge). This was finally demolished in 1825, and during the next five years, the present building designed by John Dobson, was erected on its new site. Built in the Gothic style, complete with flying buttresses and pinnacles and an unusual tower pierced by large bell openings, the Church has been improved throughout the years, while preserving its original structure.

The St. Thomas Chapel Charity, set up in 1978, administers the Trust fund for the Church, which is without its own parish.

4. THE CIVIC CENTRE
Newcastle upon Tyne

Just two miles from the busy metropolitan life of Newcastle upon Tyne, Jesmond Dene lies in its tranquil setting; a narrow wooded valley running north from Benton Bank to South Gosforth. It was acquired in the 1850's by William George Armstrong (later Lord Armstrong), who carried out extensive work, clearing and replanting exotic trees and shrubs, laying paths and building bridges. In 1883 he presented the main area of the Dene to the Corporation of Newcastle ''for the benefit of its citizens'' and in 1884 the park was formally opened by the then Prince and Princess of Wales. To commemorate the occasion the Princess planted a Turkey Oak near to the superb Banqueting Hall built by John Dobson. The park was extended in 1936 when the Noble Estate was added.

The Armstrong Bridge, dating from about 1900, is the scene each Sunday throughout the summer for a colourful local art and craft market.

Throughout the Dene there are several historic buildings including the magnificent Craghall house from about 1820, and the remains of the Chapel of Our Lady of Jesmond, probably built by the Grenville Family, one time Lords of Jesmond, early in the 12th century.

Just past the North Lodge is the spectacular waterfall with its bridge and ruined mill, the latter dating back to the 13th century. Along the river glide mute swans, mallards and moor hens, and the Dene has a special Pets Corner which is a firm favourite with all its visitors.

The Recreation and Leisure Department of Newcastle upon Tyne, together with the Friends of Jesmond Dene produce several interesting pamphlets with which you can follow History and Nature Trails through the park.

5. JESMOND DENE
Newcastle upon Tyne

TYNEMOUTH.

High on the jutting headland above the River Tyne, bounded by impressive cliffs, stand the ruins of Tynemouth Priory and Castle. There has been a monastic settlement here since the early 7th century, but repeatedly attacked by the Danes, it was not until the Normans arrived that the Priory was rebuilt by the Benedictines of Durham. Heavily fortified during the Scottish Wars, it became a rest house for numerous monarchs travelling north, and after the dissolution of the monasteries, a royal castle.

The fortified 14th century Gatehouse and Wall, approached by a road winding round a very steeply banked dry moat, guard the entrance to the site. Stormed by the Parliamentarians during the Civil War, but later restored, both the Castle and the Priory are now in the care of the English Heritage Commission and open to the public. Of particular note is the 15th century Percy Chantry, still complete, at the east end of the church, with its marvellous vaulted ceiling containing over thirty magnificently carved roof bosses.

At the foot of the cliffs is the well sheltered Prior's Haven, a small sandy bay which makes an ideal base for fishing and sailing enthusiasts. Nearby, dominating the mouth of the river, is the statue erected to Admiral Lord Collingwood, who took over at the Battle of Trafalgar after Nelson's death. Offshore are the dangerous 'Black Middens', a group of rocks that have brought disaster to many ships, and because of this the area has long associations with sea rescue. The Tynemouth Volunteer Life Brigade formed in 1865 is still in force under the command of H. M. Coastguard. A new Coastguard Station was officially opened by Prince Charles in 1985.

6. TYNEMOUTH

A picturesque harbour for the coal trade and later used by local fishermen, Cullercoats lies at the northern end of the 'Long Sands' between Tynemouth and Whitley Bay.

Few of the single-storey fishermen's cottages now survive, or their famous coble boats, but the sweep of the bay remains as hauntingly beautiful as when the fishing trade made Cullercoats a bustling port choked with boats eager to unload their catch. Then the high point of the year was mid-June to mid-July when the herring shoals were off the Tyne.

The Cullercoats Fisherwives would load up their wicker baskets on the jetties and hawk the fish around the surrounding streets crying:

"caller herrin' mussels, crabs, Hinny!"

Before the second world war they were a familiar sight on the streets of Newcastle, having travelled there on the passenger trains from the old Tynemouth Station.

Their distinctive costume of a serge dress with tucks around the lower hem and black shawl tight over the bodice appears in many paintings and photographs of the period, and is immortalised in the 'Wooden Dolly' statue. This now stands in Northumberland Square, North Shields near the

Central Library. Her predecessor, made of wood, once stood near the North Shields fish quays, but was completely eroded due to the habit of local fishermen of carving pieces from the statue to take to sea with them for luck!

7. CULLERCOATS

ST. MARY'S ISLAND.

This is a familiar landmark to visitors, situated just north of Whitley Bay. From Curry's Point, a concrete causeway gives a safe crossing to the island for three hours on each side of low tide. The island seems originally to have been known as 'Bait', 'Bates' or 'Hartley Bates Island' after a local prominent family of the time, and prior to 1855, to have been a haunt for smugglers.

At the end of the causeway steps lead to the gate of the 126 feet tall lighthouse. In medieval times a chapel dedicated to St. Helen occupied the site but all trace of it has vanished. All such coastal chapels displayed guiding lights for sailors known as 'Our Lady's Lights', or 'St. Mary's Lights', from which the island now takes its name.

The present white lighthouse was erected between 1897 and 1898 and remains the predominent feature of the island. When its construction was taking place, a graveyard containing remains of shipwrecked mariners was moved, and reburied at Seaton Delaval. The lighthouse was closed in 1984, but a local appeal to raise funds is hopeful of purchasing it from Trinity House and using it as a centre for a Natural History Museum and field studies.

On a clear day, there are splendid views from the island along the coast beyond Blyth to Lynemouth, and south to Tynemouth and as far as the Souter Lighthouse on the cliffs at Marsden.

Back across the causeway, the nearby holiday resort of Whitley Bay offers stretches of fine sandy beaches, and excellent recreational facilities for the visitor, including the Spanish City Amusement Complex, a Leisure Pool and Ice Rink.

8. ST. MARY'S ISLAND

WARKWORTH.

Ideally enter the village from the north, crossing the new bridge close to the 14th century fortified Gatehouse - the outer defence of Warkworth. The main street turns up hill, and Warkworth Castle appears outlined starkly against the sky. Enclosed in a winding loop of the River Coquet, it occupies an excellent stronghold position.

The original motte and bailey construction was erected by Henry, Earl of Northumberland in 1139. The Gatehouse, Carrickfergus and West Postern Towers were all added before 1332 when it was awarded to Henry, second Lord Percy of Alnwick.

Maintained as the Percy Family home until the 17th century when they withdrew to Alnwick, Warkworth then fell into some disrepair, but the Norman Keep and some very fine medieval masonry survives. Students of Shakespeare can relive the scenes of Harry Hotspur's conspiracy against the King which are set here. (Henry IV).

About one mile upstream from the castle is the fascinating Warkworth Hermitage carved out of solid sandstone rock. Constructed in the 14th century, romantic local legend claims the chapel was hewn by a hermit (previously a knight) in penance for a crime of passion. Above the doorway a Latin inscription (translated) reads:

"My tears have been my meat day and night"

In use until about the end of the 16th century, the Hermitage and also the Castle are now in the care of the English Heritage Commission and open to the public.

9. WARKWORTH

ALNWICK.

Situated halfway between Newcastle upon Tyne and Berwick on Tweed is this delightful historic walled town. Seat of the Percy Family, Earls of Northumberland since 1377, its many fine buildings, beautiful scenery and interesting calendar of events - notably the annual week-long costumed Medieval Fair and the International Folk Festival - attract many visitors.

It's famous castle, the backdrop for several films and T.V. series including 'King Arthur and the Spaceman' and BBC's 'Black Adder', originated in the 12th century. From 1309 it became the Percy Family stronghold and has remained with that family, now being the home of the present Duke and Duchess of Northumberland. Largely rebuilt by the first and second Percy Barons it formed a base for military operations against the Scots.

Enclosed within some seven acres of grounds landscaped by Capability Brown the castle is seen best by crossing the 'Lion Bridge' at the northern entrance to the town. The Percy Lion - a cast lead beast with it's famous stiff extended tail - also stands on the summit of the Percy Tenantry Column, locally known as 'Farmers Folly', at the southern entrance to the town.

Restored in 1750 by James Paine and Robert Adam, a second restoration in 1854 by Anthony Salvin removed much of their work, and a Renaissance style was adopted. The interior rooms of the castle are splendid and reveal a treasure house of paintings by Titan, Canaletto and Van Dyke, much fine furniture and Meissen china. Visitors may tour the Keep, Armoury, Guard Chamber, Library, Dungeon and the Museum of British and Roman Antiquities.

10. ALNWICK

DUNSTANBURGH.

One of the most impressive sights on the north east coast and described by the First Duchess of Northumberland in 1760 as "a source of glorious horror and terrible delight". The gaunt ruins of Dunstanburgh Castle are perched high on their dolomite crags at the southern end of Embleton Bay. This isolated position with a vertical drop to the sea to the north made it virtually impregnable.

Dunstanburgh occupies a site of some eleven acres, the largest area for such a building in the county, and was begun in 1313 by Thomas Earl of Lancaster. In 1322 the Earl was executed for rebelling against the King and the castle was taken in hand by Edward II, and later various Earls and Dukes of Lancaster. Important alterations, principally to turn the Gatehouse at the southern approach into a fortified Keep with portcullis, barbican and mantlet north west of it, were made in 1380 by John of Gaunt. When his son Bolingbroke usurped the crown, Dunstanburgh, as part of the Duchy of Lancaster, became a royal castle governed by a constable.

Attacked by the Scots and beseiged by the Yorkists between 1462 and 1464, by 1538 the King's Commissioners described the castle as "very ruinous". It was bought by Sir Ralph Gray of Chillingham in 1604, and remained in that family until 1869.

Now jointly administered by the English Heritage Commission and the National Trust, it provides sanctuary on its sheer northern cliffs to countless sea-birds who nest there undisturbed by cliff-top walkers. The entrance to Dunstanburgh is on the south side facing Craster, and it is open to the public.

11. DUNSTANBURGH

SEAHOUSES.

South from Bamburgh the colourful fishing villages of Seahouses and North Sunderland are set among rolling sandhills. Some sixty acres of these dunes, from Monks House to just north of the village of Seahouses, are now protected by the National Trust, having been given to them in 1936 by the First Viscount Runciman.

North Sunderland is the older of the two communities, it's name meaning 'Land to the south' (of Bamburgh), the word 'North' being added to avoid confusion with Sunderland, the large port in County Durham. Seahouses in the early 1880's was much smaller than today and consisted mainly of the fishermen's houses near the harbour, and some store houses on the higher ground behind. Hence the name 'Sea-houses' for houses beside the sea.

The fine harbour was built in the 1880's for use by vessels loading locally mined coal and lime from the kilns in the village to be exported. One lime kiln remains on the quayside, nowadays used for storing fishing gear. At the beginning of the 1890's the harbour was greatly enlarged to cater for the east coast herring boats that came here from as far afield as Scotland and Lowestoft.

At Seahouses the first kippers were smoked, and this traditional occupation is reviving following restrictions on fishing aimed at conserving stocks in the North Sea, and the subsequent decline of the industry.

Modern Seahouses, no longer separate from North Sunderland, is now establishing itself as a popular holiday centre from which sandy beaches, historic monuments and the Cheviot Hills are all easily accessible.

12. SEAHOUSES

A cluster of some twenty-eight islands lying off the coast opposite Bamburgh - the number varying with the state of the tide. Rich in history, there are two main groups: the inner and outer. The principal island, Inner Farne, about 16½ acres in extent, was the retreat of mystics for almost 900 years. The most famous was St. Cuthbert who was Prior and later Bishop of Lindisfarne and died there in 687 A.D. For centuries a place of pilgrimage, the monks built a guest house for their visitors, of which there remains the small stone 'Fishehouse'.

A dangerous area for shipping with countless boats being wrecked on the rocks, the famous Longstone Light was completed in 1826 when William Darling arrived with his family to become its first keeper. From Longstone was launched the rescue involving his daughter Grace Darling whose bravery made her a national heroine.

Today the islands have justifiably earned a reputation as one of the most fascinating bird sanctuaries in the British Isles. Their long history of bird protection began with St. Cuthbert and other early hermits who watched over nesting eider ducks. As early as 1831 birds in their breeding season were similarly guarded. The result is a wonderfully preserved natural habitat for puffins, shags, terns, kittiwakes, eider ducks and many others. Also the

only breeding place on the east coast of Britain for the Atlantic grey seal, the Farnes are a paradise for all natural history lovers.

In the care of the National Trust since 1925, trips from Seahouses visit the islands throughout the spring and summer months by motor boat.

13. FARNE ISLANDS

BAMBURGH.

A small seaside village dominated by the towering castle which rises to 150 feet above its rocky outcrop of the Great Whin Sill, and is familiar to thousands from films such as 'Becket' shot against its dramatic backdrop. From this magnificent castle the Saxon Kings ruled Northumbria throughout 'The Golden Age' when Bamburgh was the centre of chivalry, religion and learning. Its present name is a corruption of 'Bebbanburgh' after Queen Bebba, wife of Ethelfrith the first King of Northumbria.

The castle fell into decay with the decline of the Kingdom of Northumbria but was rebuilt by the Normans and survived until its surrender to the Earl of Warwick during the Wars of the Roses. James I gave it to the Forster family and it was bought by Lord Crewe, Bishop of Durham in 1704. In 1894 the first Lord Armstrong acquired the castle from the Crewe Trust and completely restored it, retaining some apartments for the use of the family. Nowadays other sections are let out as flats, and the castle is open to the public during the summer months. Visitors can tour the fine exhibitions of furniture, porcelain, arms and armour, and the Armstrong Museum.

The Grace Darling Museum in the village was opened by the Royal National Lifeboat Institution in 1938. It contains pictures, documents and relics about the nationally famous heroine, who helped to rescue the crew of the 'Forfarshire' in 1838. There is a monument to her in the local churchyard where she is buried.

14. BAMBURGH

LINDISFARNE.

A tiny isolated island about 3½ miles long, cut off from the mainland at high tide, and only accessible via a causeway over which a car can be driven at periods between the tides. Known as the 'Holy Island' and the 'Cradle of Christianity' it was here that the missionary Aidan arrived from Iona in 635 A.D. Invited by Oswald, King of Northumbria, to convert the Saxons, St. Aidan began to spread the gospel throughout the north and founded the first religious community on Lindisfarne. Most famous of the Bishops who succeeded him was St. Cuthbert, who died in 687 A.D. at his retreat on Inner Farne and was laid to rest at Lindisfarne until the monks were forced to flee in 875 A.D.

In 700 A.D. a monk of Lindisfarne named Eadfield, wrote and illustrated the world famous magnificent 'Lindisfarne Gospels' - the originals of which are now in the British Museum.

The Priory was rebuilt at the end of the 11th century by the Benedictine monks from Durham and prospered until dissolution in 1537. Its buildings were then used as a military storehouse, and some of its stone used to build a fort and castle. The red sandstone ruins point impressively skywards from their pinnacle of rock and are now in the care of the English Heritage Commission.

In 1902 Sir Edwin Lutyens rennovated the castle. It was handed to the National Trust in 1944 and is open to the public during the summer months when trips can be taken from nearby Bamburgh and Seahouses. The island is also a favourite haunt for naturalists.

15. LINDISFARNE

BERWICK ON TWEED.

An ancient Border town, the most northerly in England, whose three bridges astride the River Tweed, Berwick is one of the best examples of a fortified town in Northern Europe. Its long and chequered history, from 547 A.D. is characterised by bitter conflicts and feuds fought backwards and forwards across its land. A Scottish Royal Burgh in the 12th century it was finally established as part of England in 1482.

Little remains of the 12th century castle which was plundered for its stone, most notably by Robert Stephenson to build the famous Royal Border Bridge of 28 arches opened by Queen Victoria in 1850. The site of the castle was finally cleared to build the present Railway Station in the middle of the 19th century. The middle of the three bridges, the Royal Tweed Bridge, was opened in 1928 by the Prince of Wales (later Edward VIII), to carry the Great North Road between England and Scotland. The oldest surviving bridge, completed in 1634, has one parapet higher than the rest, which originally served to mark the boundary between Berwick and North Durham.

Excellently preserved are the Elizabethan fortifications that encircle the town. The ramparts are open to the public and from them can be viewed a rich variety of historic buildings including the Guildhall, Art Gallery Museum, Holy Trinity Church and the Georgian Custom House in the Quay Walls. Berwick Barracks, the King's Own Scottish Borderers' Regimental Museum and the earliest military barracks in England, now houses an exciting complex of exhibitions and displays.

Berwick is a bustling market town with good shopping facilities and provides an excellent start for excursions around the Border Country.

16. BERWICK ON TWEED

NORHAM.

This border stronghold was founded in 1121 by Bishop Flambard to protect a crossing point of the River Tweed and hold the land against the onslaught of the Scots. Its name comes from 'Northam' as for centuries Norham was part of the country palatine of Durham and the most northernly defence of the Bishop of Durham. The original motte and bailey structure was destroyed by David I of Scotland and the castle rebuilt later in the 12th century by Bishop Hugh de Puiset.

Attacked and battered, Norham withstood two long sieges by Robert the Bruce between 1318 and 1319. During the second of these, a Lincolnshire knight, Sir William Marmion, was sent to reinforce the garrison. So impressed by his story was Sir Walter Scott that he later made Marmion the hero of his famous epic poem, which so perfectly captures the picture of this great English fortress.

Finally stormed by the forces of James IV in 1513 and the 'Mons Meg' cannon, Norham fell into some decay but remained a Border defence until the end of the 16th century when it was considered too costly to upkeep.

In 1923 it was placed under the guardianship of the 'Commissioners of His Majesty's Works' and now in the care of the English Heritage Commission, Norham is still an impressive sight. Its massive Keep rises dramatically above the treeline and the pink sandstone walls in sunlight adopt a mellow glow echoing Sir Walter Scott's words:

''The flanking walls that round it sweep,
In yellow lustres shone''.

(Marmion)

17. NORHAM

In the Northern part of Northumberland's National Park among the finest scenery in the country, is the rolling range of the Cheviot Hills. High land since before the Ice Age, the landscape here is full of change and contrast, wild and lonely.

The hills are grass covered and from their summit many clear brooks and streams flow through the glens over a carpet of heather and ferns. The area is home to the elusive Wild Cheviot Goats and the Chillingham Wild White Cattle. Rich in ancient earthworks, there are remains of iron age forts and the dwellings of the 'Votadini', the early Pre- Roman inhabitants of Northumberland.

At 2,676 feet the Muckle Cheviot is the tallest peak in the county, a huge dome-shaped mass of grass covered granite, it lends its name to the whole range of hills. One of the first tourists to climb to its summit must have been the writer 'Daniel Defoe' in 1728, who described his journey in ''Tour through Great Britain''. A determined walker will find the easiest route up from Langlee Ford, and be rewarded by marvellous views from the top.

The chief centre for visitors to the Cheviots is Wooler, a quiet Northumbrian town, historically one of the ancient baronies from the Norman Conquest. Set in picturesque scenery with the impressive Cheviots to the west, the town houses the Cheviot Field Centre and Museum. This is a venture of the Northumberland Archaeology Group and is well equipped for a variety of outdoor activities. The Museum houses many archaeological exhibits of local interest.

18. CHEVIOT HILLS

CHILLINGHAM CATTLE.

South east of Wooler, nestling among the Cheviot Hills, is the vast natural parkland home to the Chillingham Wild White Cattle immortalised by the dramatic drawings made of them by Thomas Bewick.

The only herd of its kind in the world, they are believed to be descended from the wild ox 'Bos Taurus' which formerly roamed the forests of Northern Britain. With a history of pure breeding extending over 700 years, there is no record of any domesticated blood ever being introduced into the herd, and it is left to roam wild even when many are lost, as in the severe winter of 1947.

Not completely white, the cattle have dark eyes, muzzles and hoofs. Ruled by the King Bull, they can stampede if approached too closely by humans, and applications to see them should be made to the Warden who will accompany visitors.

Chillingham is the family seat of the Tankerville family. The 12th century St. Peter's Church in the village was restored in 1966 and houses the magnificently carved table tomb of Sir Ralph Gray and his wife.

The original castle of 1344 had four angle towers connected by a curtain wall, and was added to in the 17th and 18th centuries. Restoration work is being carried out and parts of the castle are open to the public, as are the grounds, which were landscaped about 1753 but also include a formal Elizabethan topiary garden.

19. CHILLINGHAM CATTLE

ROTHBURY.

Surrounded by some of the most beautiful scenery in Northumbria, this attractive country town lies in the heart of the Coquetdale among wooded and heather-carpeted hills. Charmingly unspoilt, its long main street, lined with trees and fronted by sturdy stone buildings, is on two levels and winds downhill to a triangular green.

All Saints Church was rebuilt in 1850 and has a 13th century Chancel and a Font made of Saxon carved shaft, believed to be part of a cross dating from about 800 A.D. Lord Armstrong, the famous engineer and inventor is buried here in the family plot not far from his splendid mansion 'Cragside' which is on the steeply rising ground to the north east of the town. On the green near the churchyard, the site of the old market cross, stands a tall cross erected to the memory of Lord Armstrong and his wife.

High on Lorbottle Crags just four miles north west of Rothbury are the ruins of the 14th century Cartington Castle, and among the nearby hills are sites of several prehistoric camps, and the ruin on an old Pele Tower at Great Tosson.

The Forestry Commission have established Nature Trails through the Simonside Hills providing delightful walks for the visitor, and the River Coquet, spanned by a medieval bridge brought up to modern specifications, is popular with keen anglers.

20. ROTHBURY

CRAGSIDE.

Just to the north of Thrum Mill, near Rothbury, is this lavishly furnished Victorian mansion designed in 1870 by Richard Norman Shaw for the first Lord Armstrong: local inventor, engineer, industrialist and armament king. Built in mock Tudor style, the house is set in a magnificent country park of 900 acres and looks down over Rothbury and Coquetdale to the Simonsides.

Local opinion expressed at the time reads:

"And on your brown and rocky hill see princely Cragside lies.
Where boundless wealth and perfect taste have made a paradise".

The grounds, a happy blend of woodland and formal gardens contain enormous banks of superb rhododendrons, several million trees planted by Lord Armstrong, lakes, a gorge and waterfalls. Miles of pathways meander through the parkland revealing many spectacular views.

Cragside was the first house in the world to be lit by electricity generated by its own water power, and examples of the early scientific apparatus used by Lord Armstrong and his friend and co-worker, the inventor Joseph Swan, are preserved. A hydraulic lift and spit, devised by Lord Armstrong for domestic convenience, also survive.

The house contains much of the original furniture, Pre-Raphaelite paintings from the De-Morgan Collection and fine William Morris glass. Cragside house and grounds are now in the care of the National Trust and open to the public throughout the year.

21. CRAGSIDE

KIELDER.

Western Europe's largest man-made lake has a surface area of 2,684 acres, is seven and a half miles long with a maximum depth of 170 feet. It can yield up to 200 million gallons of water a day and connects the natural drainage systems at the rivers Tyne, Wear and Tees by an aquaduct to form a regional water supply grid. Situated in the huge Border Forest Park of the Upper Tyne Valley, Kielder is designed to meet the region's water supply needs into the next century.

With far-sighted planning and careful exploitation of natural resources in the area, Kielder also provides a vast aqua-leisure complex catering for many outdoor interests and recreational pursuits. The activities run by the Kielder Water Club include dinghy sailing, wind surfing, canoeing, water skiing, and sail or motor cruising. There is also provision for caravanning, camping, pony trekking, orienteering and bird watching. From the four Activity Centres within the complex guided tours and professional tuition in sports are available.

A twelve mile long Forest Drive from Kielder Castle to Byrness reveals spectacular views and secluded picnic areas. The Forest is the scene annually of the famous Lombard RAC Motor Rally.

The north shore of the lake has been left a wild area, cars are not allowed there leaving it free for footpaths, bridleways and undisturbed wildlife. A nature conservation site has been created on the south shore of Bakethin Reservoir to help protect its wide variety of plants and wildlife. Visitors can overlook it from an elevated viewpoint on the famous skewed arch viaduct at Kielder.

The Foresty Commission have established an Information Centre at Kielder Castle, once the Duke of Northumberland's shooting lodge, and at Tower Knowe is the Water Operations Centre.

22. KIELDER

ROMAN WALL.

Built following a visit to Britain by the Emperor Hadrian in 122 A.D., this was the northern frontier of the Roman Empire in Britain and meant to separate the Romans from the Barbarians. An awesome complex of installations, it stretched for 80 Roman miles from Wallsend on Tyne to Bowness on Solway.

Not only a line of defence, the Wall was in fact a massive communications system, with 17 forts along its length, and milecastles situated at one Roman mile distance between which were signal towers. As an additional strategy, a deep v-shaped ditch was dug close to the north side, and to the south was the Vallum, a broader flat-bottomed ditch marking the boundary of the military zone, and serving as a supply route.

The four miles of the Wall from Housesteads to Steel Rigg in the central section, are in the care of the National Trust. At the fort of Housesteads, from which are breathtaking views along the Wall, are some fascinating remains of Roman life. These include an example of a hospital, a well-preserved latrine system, and the museum, itself a reconstruction of a vicus building, which displays items excavated from the site.

Able to accommodate 1,000 infantry Housteads was occupied by the First Cohort from Belgium, and fully manned the Wall would have been garrisoned by at least 13,000 men. By 400 A.D. however, the Roman Empire was nearing collapse and all these men were withdrawn home. Over the next 1,500 years farmers needing building materials, animals seeking shelter, and the builders of the 'Military Road' (B6318) all plundered the Wall. Despite these and other losses, long stretches remain intact and are being preserved, and the remains stand as a unique example of Roman culture.

23. ROMAN WALL

VINDOLANDA.

Once the frontier home for 500 Roman Auxiliary soldiers, Vindolanda lies just to the south of Hadrian's Wall between Houseteads and Great Chesters, and the earliest remains date from 90 A.D. Excavations have uncovered part of the 4th century fort and the heart of the civilian settlement which lay outside the walls.

The unusual preservative properties in the soil have meant that many of the objects uncovered are in a wonderfully undamaged condition. Many varieties of coins, pots, clothing and writing tablets have been found, and the full-time research staff are continually making new and exciting discoveries on the site.

A wealth of these Roman artefacts are attractively displayed in the museum which is housed in the country house of Chesterholm set in its own charming gardens. Here the vivid audio-visual displays and reconstructions bring to life the atmosphere of Roman times. Similarly outside, replica Roman Walls (full scale) and a timber milecastle gateway, give an idea of the original strength and power of the Fort and Walls.

The Headquarters Building was the largest and most important at the fort. Near the entrance of this administrative centre were rooms to store weapons and uniforms. In an open courtyard beyond is a well which when first excavated revealed wood and leather items and oxen skulls. The Crosshall with its rostrum is where the men would assemble to be addressed by their commanding officer. Other rooms include the Chapel of the Standards, offices and a strong-room.

The Vindolanda Trust is a registered archaeological Charity who continue to work on the site, and both the buildings and the museum are open to the public.

24. VINDOLANDA:
    HEADQUARTERS BUILDING

HEXHAM.

The administrative centre for Tynedale District, and enjoying an attractive position in beautiful countryside, Hexham has survived a long and turbulent history. Ravaged and sacked by the Danes, burned and pillaged by the Scots, and the scene of a tragic riot against the local militia in 1761, it survives as the 'Heart of West Northumberland' -an ideal centre from which to tour the many unspoilt villages, castles and fortified towers in the neighbourhood, and also a busy market town. The most important building is Hexham Church or Abbey, which dominates the Market Place and whose bell used to call the inhabitants to arms when raiders appeared. Founded in 673 A.D., parts of the Saxon crypt remain virtually intact built from Roman stones, many of them carved with ornaments and inscriptions. The existing church, begun in the 12th century, has extremely fine examples of Chancel and Transepts. In the centre of the Chancel stands St. Wilfrid's Chair, tub-shaped and about 1,300 years old, it once stood in the original Anglo-Saxon Church and is also known as the Frith Stool, from the time when sanctuary could be claimed by sitting in it.

Also of note are the 13th century Moot Hall and the 14th century Manor Office, the latter now serves as the Middlemarch Centre for Border History, and contains the Tourist Information Centre.

The long nine-arched bridge over the River Tyne, designed by Robert Mylne in 1785, offers a good viewpoint over the whole of the town, and the nearby Hexham Tyne Green Country Park with its charming river and hillside walks.

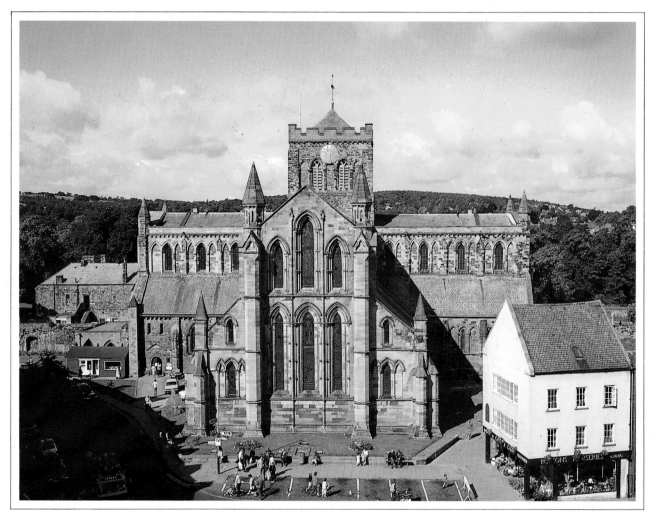

25. HEXHAM

CORBRIDGE.

An historic riverside town some four miles east of Hexham on the north bank of the Tyne. Corbridge came to prominence in A.D. 81 when the Romans developed it as a strategic crossing point of the river, although there is some evidence of occupation of the site from early Bronze Age times. For nearly a century it was a base for a sequence of Roman forts at the junction of roads leading to Scotland, York and Carlisle, and attracted a large civilian settlement.

There is a wealth of historic buildings to fascinate the visitor. The Anglo-Saxon Church of St. Andrew stands in the Market Place. Vicar's Pele, which houses the Tourist Information Centre is a prime example of a Northumbrian Pele Tower.

To the west of the town is the excavated Roman station of 'Corstopitum' first uncovered between 1906 and 1914. The main buildings include two buttressed granaries, a fountain fed by an aquaduct, an enormous storehouse, small temples and numerous shops and houses for those who supplied the garrison. A museum displays a fine collection of sculptures, the most famous being the Corbridge Lion - a lion devouring a stag -models of the camp and artefacts found at the site.

A charmingly unhurried market town, Corbridge is a convenient centre from which to explore other important sections of the Roman Wall. Set amid some attractive countryside, to the south west of the town there are delightful woodland walks along the banks of 'Devils Water' - the setting for the famous Anya Seton novel of the same name.

26. CORBRIDGE

STEPHENSON'S COTTAGE

10 miles from Newcastle on the north bank of the Tyne, and once a famous colliery village, Wylam is well-known as the birthplace of early steam engines. The 'Puffing Billy', first of these engines, was designed here and put into use between Wylam and the Lemington Staithes. Its creator, William Hedley is remembered by a memorial in the village church of St. Oswin.

But it is with the name of George Stephenson, the world famous engineer and inventor, that Wylam is most closely associated. He was born here on 9th June 1781 in High St. House, a stone built dwelling with a red pantile roof, outside which ran the wooded tramway laid in 1748 to take coal in horse-drawn waggons from Wylam to Lemington Staithes. The Stephenson family lived there until 1789. In 1808 the timber tracks outside the cottage were replaced with iron plate and in 1876 North Wylam station was opened to serve as a loop of the Newcastle-Carlisle Railway and was in operation until 1968. The Waggonway is now preserved by Northumberland County Council as a riverside walk, and Stephenson's birthplace is in the care of the National Trust.

George Stephenson built his first engine 'Blucher' in 1814, and in 1818 formed a partnership with Edward Pease which resulted in their obtaining an Act of Parliament to construct a railway from Witton Colliery to Stockton On Tees.

On 27th September, 1825 Stephenson's 'Locomotion Number One' pulled the first passenger train at 14 miles an hour, opening the world famous Stockton to Darlington railway.

This was followed in 1830 by the opening of the Liverpool to Manchester Railway when Stephenson's engine the 'Rocket' hauled the waggons.

Stephenson himself died in 1848 and is buried in Trinity Church, Chesterfield.

27. STEPHENSON'S COTTAGE
Wylam

MORPETH.

A market town in the Wansbeck Valley, its river is crossed by a 13th century footbridge, and the one constructed in 1831 by Thomas Telford to carry the Great North Road. Morpeth, meaning ''the path over the moor'' has long been associated with travellers going north, who were in part responsible for its growth. Happily now by-passed by the A1 road, Morpeth remains a solid and prosperous country town.

Its shopping streets still retain some 18th century facades and the well-known 15th century Clock Tower - once a house of correction and famous for sounding a nightly curfew - is well preserved. Vanbrugh's impressive Town Hall was rebuilt following the fire of 1869.

Down an avenue of trees with a screen of columns and arches is St. James Church, built in 1846 by Benjamin Ferrey. The fine old parish church of St. Mary's is mostly 14th century, with some Norman additions, and is one of the largest parish churches in Northumberland. At Oldgate in the town, lived Admiral Lord Collingwood, Nelson's deputy at Trafalgar.

The ruins of Morpeth Castle, standing on Castle Hill consist of a well-preserved Gatehouse, now a private residence. Opposite is the huge battlemented Courthouse and police station built in 1822 by the Newcastle architect John Dobson.

Morpeth is justly proud of its beautifully maintained parks, and delightful walks and excursions can be taken along the banks of the River Wansbeck.

28. MORPETH

WALLINGTON HALL.

About twenty miles from the Roman Wall in the 'Middle Marches' of Northumberland, a land famous in Border Ballads, is this 17th century mansion within a wooded parkland. Its East Front is guarded by stone griffin heads brought from Bishopgate in London and placed in their present position in 1928.

The main approach is over Paine's Bridge built by him in 1755 to cross the River Wansbeck. Once the moorland stronghold of the Fenwick Clan, the only remains of that castle are in the cellars of the present Hall.

The original late 17th century house was completely remodelled by Sir Walter Calverley Blackett, a powerful Newcastle merchant and local owner of coal and lead mines. Passed to the descendants of his sister who married a Trevelyan, through their influence it became associated with artists, writers, scientists and politicians.

The Central Hall, by Dobson, was decorated by William Bell Scott and John Ruskin among others. The interior of the house is remarkable for the fine 18th century craftsmanship in wood, marble and plaster. A treasure store of beautiful period furniture, ceramics, rococo plasterwork, Pre-Raphaelite wall paintings, and the famous Wallington Collection of Dolls' Houses.

The Clock Tower is one of the most appealing architectural features, originally designed as a Chapel and built in 1754, it houses a display of carriages, a restaurant and a shop.

The walled garden, half a mile from the house is a delight to explore, entered by the Neptune Gate, a pool and water garden are revealed. Both the Hall and the Gardens, now owned by the National Trust, are open to the public.

29. WALLINGTON HALL

THE PORT OF TYNE.

The Tyne today is greatly changed from the gentle, shallow river that flowed through Northumbria, past picturesque islands, and teamed with plentiful shoals of fish. The upper reaches of the river and its main tributaries, the North and South Tyne, still travel through the same enchanting countryside and have altered the least, but the increasing world wide demand for coal hastened the development of the port.

From the 13th century coal was shipped from the Tyne but as trade grew and ships became larger, the problems of navigation at the entrance to the river, then unprotected and extremely dangerous in bad weather, demanded attention. In 1850 legislation created the Tyne Improvement Commission charged with making the river safe and navigable, and providing facilities for the increasing seaborne traffic.

In 1854 the construction of the North and South Piers of solid masonry was begun and they were completed in their present form in 1909. Now a familiar landmark whose long grey arms snake out to encircle the river, they enable the port to remain open in all weathers creating a harbour refuge with access to safe shipping berths. The Commission also organised the building of Northumberland Dock, Albert Edward Dock and the Swing Bridge.

The Port of Tyne Authority, set up by the Ministry of Transport in 1968, now controls these facilities together with those provided by the Corporations of Newcastle upon Tyne, Gateshead, and Tynemouth.

Tyneside, with its continuing river development, can deal with oil imports and welcome today's largest bulk carriers, whilst maintaining its traditional passenger ferry links with Scandinavia.

30. THE PORT OF TYNE

A superb panorama of the City, dominated by the Cathedral and the Castle, can be seen by rail travellers crossing the great Victorian viaduct into Durham station.

The magnificent Norman Cathedral, one of the best known features of Northumbria's Christian heritage, is acclaimed as the finest example of its kind in the world. Together with the Castle, it occupies an impressive position which came to play a strategic role in history:

"half Church of God, half Castle 'gainst the Scot".
(Sir Walter Scott)

The story of Durham spans a thousand years beginning with the followers of St. Cuthbert. Forced to flee their original home on Lindisfarne, legend states that they were led here in 995 A.D. by a vision. The monks erected a small church to house the relics of their Saint. The Normans, realising the potential of Durham as a defensive stronghold, founded the Castle and replaced the little church with the present Cathedral. St. Cuthbert's shrine can still be seen beneath the immense and elegant vaulting of the Cathedral, and his original wooden coffin and other relics can be viewed in the Cathedral Treasury.

For over 800 years the Castle was the home of the Prince Bishops of Durham, who were not only religious leaders, but rulers second only to the Crown, having their own army, courts, nobility and coinage.

Today the Castle is part of Durham's eminent University, England's third oldest after Oxford and Cambridge. The narrow twisting medieval streets survive as part of the busy shopping centre.

31. DURHAM CITY

DURHAM CATHEDRAL.

Viewed from the banks of the River Wear the Cathedral is entirely framed in woodland green, a scene which has hardly changed since the Middle Ages.

Deservedly renowned as one of the finest examples of Norman architecture, it owes much of its splendour to the fact that the main structure: the nave, chancel and transepts, were created in a single period between 1070 and 1140. Also important for its startling structural innovations which include the pointed arches across the nave, the first of their kind in English architectural history, and the ribbed vaulting of the roof - the earliest known in the West. These features were to become hallmarks of Gothic architecture in later generations.

A climb up the 325 steps of the Central Tower is rewarded with a bird's eye view of the tightly knit medieval streets which cling to the lower slopes of the peninsula, almost encircled by the river, on which the Cathedral stands.

The Old Fulling Mill on the riverside has been converted into an Archaeological Museum. On display are exhibits dating from the Stone Age to Saxon times, taken from excavations in and around Durham. The wooded river banks provide a beautiful setting for walking, fishing or boating, and each June witnesses what is reputed to be the oldest rowing regatta in the world.

For centuries a place of pilgrimage, Durham today hosts visitors from around the world who come to experience the romantic atmosphere of the City, and explore its rich and varied heritage.

32. DURHAM CATHEDRAL

ST. PAUL'S CHURCH.

Half a mile east of modern Jarrow, travelling towards South Shields, is the almost hidden site of St. Paul's Church. Founded by Bishop Benedict in 681 A.D., the Venerable Bede lived and worked here for over half a century and it is also known as St. Bede's Monastery. Whilst at Jarrow Bede wrote some fifty ecclesiastical works including translating the Bible into English. His most well-known and authoritative work is 'The History of the English Church and People' which relates the early Saxon development in Northumbria.

In the three centuries after Bede the monastery was twice sacked by the Danes and was later destroyed by William the Conqueror. In 1069 A.D. Aldwin, Prior of Winchcombe, came north with companions to rebuild the community and monastic life continued at Jarrow until the dissolution of the monasteries in 1536.

A new nave was built in 1782 which was replaced in 1866 by the present one, designed by Sir Gilbert Scott. The outlines of the second monastery of Prior Aldwin are still visible at the southern exterior of the site.

At the east end of the original Saxon chapel built with Roman stone survives as the chancel of the present church. An ancient chair, known as 'St. Bede's Chair' may also date from Saxon times.

Above the tower arch is the original dedication stone, still bearing its Latin inscription marking the date: 23rd April 681 A.D.

Close-by Jarrow Hall's 'Bede Monastery Museum' tells the story of Northumbrian Saxon monastic life with displays, models, excavated finds and audio-visual presentations.

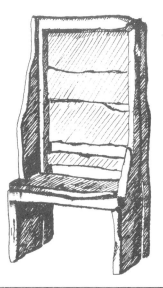

33. ST. PAUL'S CHURCH
Jarrow

73

South along the coast from South Shields is Marsden Bay, where offshore stand the impressive Marsden Rocks. These huge vertical-sided stacks, one of which is known as 'Lot's Wife', were once part of the main cliffs. The sea has eroded the softer limestone to form first caves, then arches, and finally the structures to be seen today. Teaming with sea birds, the rocks are now important nesting sites for fulmars and kittiwakes, and a roosting area for cormorants. Because of their presence the area attracts bird-watchers and natural history enthusiasts.

The 'Marsden Grotto' is a fascinating feature of this part of the coast which is romantically linked with the activities of smugglers in local legends. In 1782 a miner working at the Marsden Quarry came to live with his family in a cave at the foot of the cliffs. He built stairs into the rock to reach his home which are still known as 'Jack the Blaster' stairs.

Later the cave was taken over by Peter Allen, son of Sir Hedworth Williamson's gamekeeper, who enlarged and developed it, building out a front, and driving a vertical shaft into the cliff down which supplies could be lowered. In the course of his excavations in 1836 he unearthed four skeletons of men who had met violent deaths, thus adding to the stories circulating locally about smugglers. After his death in the 1850's, his club became a popular haunt of artists and writers. Today there is still a public house and restaurant at Marsden Grotto, which can be reached by a lift from the cliff-top.

Nearby, at Lizard Point, stands the well-known landmark of Souter Lighthouse. Built in 1871 it was so named to avoid confusion with Lizard Point Lighthouse in Cornwall.

34. MARSDEN

WASHINGTON OLD HALL.

Less than two miles from the A1(M) motorway in the village of Washington, County Durham, is the home of the ancestors of George Washington, who became the First President of the United States of America in 1789.

A small manor house, originally built in the 12th century of local sandstone, it became the property of the 'de Wessyngton' (later Washington) family in 1183, and stayed with their descendants until 1613. Standing partly on the 12th century foundations and retaining some of their outer walls at the West end, it was largely rebuilt in 1610.

George Washington's grandfather emigrated to America in 1656 taking with him his family coat-of-arms, which as it contained stars and stripes, has led to the suggestion that it was the inspiration of 'Old Glory', the American flag. Although this is considered unlikely by many, the Stars and Stripes is flown from the flagpole on the South Terrace on the three American Festivals: 22nd Feb., 4th July and 23rd Nov.

Saved from demolition in 1936 by a local Preservation Committee the house was restored by them with the help of funds from both sides of the Atlantic. Officially opened by the American Ambassador in 1955, it passed into the care of the National Trust a couple of years later. The Trust together with Friends of the property have chosen and furnished the interior in the style of a typical 17th century manor house; and laid out the gardens, both of which are open to the public.

35. WASHINGTON OLD HALL

BEAMISH MUSEUM.

Easily reached from the Chester-le-Street turn-off of the A1(M), Beamish near Stanley is the North of England's premier open-air museum. Here can be seen a remarkable re-creation of North East life as it was around eighty years ago. Buildings have been painstakingly transported stone by stone from their original sites, and re-constructed here.

There is Rowley Station of 1867 with its passenger platform, goods depot, signal box, weigh cabin and waiting room, all in working order, and from where in the summer steam trains leave to tour the Museum.

Nearby is the cobbled town street of Ravensworth Terrace, fitted out and furnished as it would have been in the 1920's, and down which rattles an electric tramcar. The buildings include a dentist's surgery, solicitor's office, a middle class home, and the Victorian Public House: the Sun Inn. Across the street is the Co-operative Store, brought here from Annfield Plain near Consett, full of fascinating 1920's merchandise in its grocery, drapery and hardware departments.

In the colliery area there are trips underground down 'Mahogany Drift' where an ex-pitman will demonstrate how coal was mined by hand. A terrace of pitmen's cottages, Francis Street, are furnished traditionally and the art of bread making and the construction of 'proggy' mats are demonstrated.

As well as pigs, ducks and hens at the Home Farm Beamish is helping to preserve a growing herd of Durham short-horn cattle.

Open all the year round, the Museum is administered by a consortium of four north-east County Councils.

36. BEAMISH MUSEUM

The idea and benefaction of the son of the 10th Earl of Strathmore, John Bowes and his French wife, Josephine Benoite, the museum is situated in the market town of Barnard Castle at the east end of Newgate, just four miles from the A66. It was built here as the nearest convenient site to John Bowes' ancestral home, Streatlam Castle, which is now demolished.

Designed in 1869 by the French architect, Jules Pellechet, Bowes Museum is some 300 feet long and 120 feet wide with large terraces and pavilions and was built to resemble a French chateau. Finally opened in 1892, it houses one of the finest collections of art in England, brought together during the period 1840 to 1870.

There are fine examples of British and French decorative arts, pottery, porcelain, embroideries and tapestries, and a Music Gallery containing a rare collection of musical instruments. The Picture Gallery reveals a magnificent display of paintings by El Greco, Goya and Canaletto. The superb Costume Gallery was opened by H.M. Queen Mother in 1976.

From the Entrance Hall portraits of John Bowes and his wife look down on visitors, and their lives and activities are detailed in an exhibition in the Founders Room.

The Museum is set in 20 acres of landscaped gardens, including a formal garden in the French style, and contains almost one hundred varieties of trees.

In 1956 the Trustees handed the Museum and its contents over to Durham County Council, and it remains in their care and is open to the public.

37. BOWES MUSEUM

FINCHALE PRIORY.

The romantic ruins of the Priory stand in a loop of the meandering River Wear, encircled on three sides by its bright water, and two miles east of Plawsworth off the A167 between Durham and Chester-le-Street. Built on the site of the hermitage of St. Godric, legend states he was directed here in a dream by St. Cuthbert.

At first living in a rough shelter, Godric then built the small timber chapel of St. Mary. In later years a second stone chapel dedicated to St. John the Baptist was erected, and here against the north wall, St Godric's tomb lies.

After his death the buildings passed into the care of the Prior of Durham and Benedictine monks settled there. The Priory was rebuilt about 1237 but by 1364 was considerably scaled down with the aisles of the 13th century church blocked and the south aisle of the nave becoming the north cloister walk. During the 14th century Finchale began to be used as a holiday retreat for monks which continued until it was abandoned at the dissolution of the lesser monasteries in 1536.

Among the interesting remains the walls of the Chancel still stand almost to their original height, and the extensive ruins of the domestic quarters give a fascinating insight into early monastic life.

Now in the care of the English Heritage Commission, the Priory is open to the public, and there are picturesque riverside walks nearby and facilities for visitors.

38. FINCHALE PRIORY

The River Tees, born high in the barren remote Pennines on the Cumbrian-Durham border, flows through rugged hills little changed since prehistoric times. Here amidst the picturesque Pennine Dales, an area famous both for its Lead Mining heritage and its attractive countryside and villages, is the Upper Teesdale Nature Reserve. Now incorporating the area of Widdybank Fell to the east, the reserve also includes the banks of the river between Cauldron Snout and High Force waterfalls. The scenic beauty here is dramatic, and below Cow Green Reservoir the River Tees tumbles through a rocky chasm in a series of cataracts.

Two miles from the Reservoir along a wooded walk, is High Force, the biggest waterfall in Northern England. Bounded by grim walls of black basalt with vertical joints resting on layers of mountain limestone, the waterfall rushes down a wide rocky channel of the Whin Sill. A huge iron-brown rock is breached by the river, and water plunges 70 feet downwards into a deep swirling pool. Even in moderate flow it is an impressive sight, but in full spate the thunderous roar is almost deafening.

(The Tees)
"and rushing madly headlong o'er
At High Force leaps with ceaseless roar
Thence bubbling, hissing, onward goes".

(Sir Walter Scott)

High Force is part of the vast private Raby Estate, situated on the B6277 Middleton-in-Teesdale to Alston road, and can be visited by the public.

39. HIGH FORCE WATERFALL

SUNDERLAND.

The chief port of County Durham situated on an estuary of the River Wear, its safe harbours and dock accommodation established Sunderland as an important shipping area early in its history. Although it maintains industrial and shipbuilding traditions, the town has a rich heritage, and its excellent modern leisure facilities and attractive coastline make it a popular resort for visitors. Its sheltered marina is the base for local boating and sailing enthusiasts.

Historically, coal mining and glassmaking are centred here, the first glaziers bringing glass from Gaul for the original monastery of St. Peter at Monkwearmouth. Founded in 674 A.D., the Venerable Bede spent his early life there, and it became one of the important seats of learning in the early English church. Its square Saxon tower is still in use as a Parish Church.

The Crowtree Leisure Centre, one of the largest in the country, has several thousand visitors a year to its ice-rink and swimming pool, and is home to the Sunderland Maestros Basketball Club. A full programme of exhibitions, competitions and conferences take place there annually. At Silksworth a former colliery site, is a vast open-air recreational complex with a dry ski-slope, all-weather pitches and fishing facilities.

Close-by are the twin resorts of Roker and Seaburn sharing two miles of sandy beaches, the former being the home of the Sunderland Football Club.

Dominating the skyline to the north of Sunderland, is the famous Penshaw Monument, a reproduction of a Greek temple, built in 1844 to honour the first Earl of Durham.

40. SUNDERLAND MARINA

Index

Also Published by Sandhill Press

THE BORDER REIVERS by Godfrey Watson.
Who were the 'Reivers': gallant adventurers or blood-thirsty cattle thieves? Godfrey Watson trace their exciting story through this colourful description of 16th century life in the ''Land of Romance'' - the border between Scotland and England.

GOODWIFE HOT AND OTHERS: Northumberland's past as shown in its place names by Godfrey Watson.
How did a hill fortress come to be called 'Goodwife Hot' or a farm 'Pity Me'? Through these and other names of towns and villages, farms and shepherds' huts, the fascinating history of Northumberland is revealed.

NORTHUMBRIAN Views: six selected 18th and 19th century watercolours.
Reproduced from the Laing Art Gallery and Tyne & Wear County Council's collection of important watercolours.

The publishers are always interested to hear from anyone who has local material for publication, or wishes to suggest titles to be reprinted.